A BOOT UP

DEVON'S JURASSIC COAST

Rodney Legg

First published in Great Britain in 2009

British Library Cataloguing-in-Publication Data
A CIP record for this title is available from the British Library

ISBN 978 1 906887 20 9

PiXZ Books
Halsgrove House, Ryelands Industrial Estate,
Bagley Road, Wellington, Somerset TA21 9PZ
Tel: 01823 653777
Fax: 01823 216796
email: sales@halsgrove.com

An imprint of Halstar Ltd, part of the Halsgrove group of companies
Information on all Halsgrove titles is available at: www.halsgrove.com

Printed and bound by Grafiche Flaminia, Italy

Contents

Introduction

The Area

Iron-staining has given us the warm pinks and reds of Devon's sandstone cliffs. These were laid down 240 million years ago in warm lagoons when Britain's tectonic plate, floating on the Earth's mantle, was 15 degrees further south at the same latitude as the modern Sahara. This continental drift - causing Africa to collide into Europe - led to the uplifting that produced the remarkable landform geology of the East Devon and Dorset coast. From Orcombe Point to Old Harry Rocks it was designated as a World Heritage Site by Unesco in 2001. You can time travel, literally, as the rocks get younger from west to east to span 185 million years in 95 miles.

The mid-Triassic and other sandstones from 250 million years ago reach their maximum extent between High Peak and Danger Point where they are up to 120 metres thick. There is a wide range of plant, amphibian, fish and reptile fossils, with the notable local dinosaur being the Rhynchosaur. This barrel-shaped vegetarian had a double row of upper teeth into which sharper bottom teeth fitted for a chopping action to crush sea ferns.

Lakes around Axmouth were surrounded by a desert 210 million years ago. The geology now tells us more, in that some of these cliffs are topped with chalk from the Cretaceous period (110 million years ago here, though solid white cliffs between Swanage and Studland are much younger, at 65 million years old).

Devon meets Dorset with a flourish. Chalk is wholly fossil in that it comprises the calcium carbonate from trillions of minute sea creatures.

Layers of inorganic matter became lumps of flint. Beyond the glint of Devon's white cliffs are the most spectacularly fossiliferous beds of all, in the Blue Lias of the Jurassic, yielding iconic specimens of ammonite and Ichthyosaur. The noticeable change in the colour of the rocks - from red to green and grey - indicates that they were laid down in less arid conditions.

Behind these coastal exposures the landscape rises and falls into a series of deep-cut valleys between high plateaus of wild or wooded pebbled-heaths. Their equivalent of flint is called chert. Between the hills run the rivers that provide the root elements for many place-names - being from west to east the Exe, Otter, Sid and Axe. Present-day harbours are at Exmouth and Axmouth. Former quays were at Budleigh Salterton and around the corner in the Otter Estuary where the tidal river was navigable to Otterton. Shrubby sea purslane now grows on mudflats across the site of these moorings which are managed for the fauna and flora (notably the otters you might expect from its name) by Devon Wildlife Trust.

The Routes

All routes are circular - meaning they bring you back to the starting point - and are of moderate length. They vary from four to eleven miles and are graded from one to three boots - from easy to the more challenging. They are ideal for families or groups of friends looking for an afternoon in glorious historic countryside or for a more leisurely walk with a suitable pause at a pub or refreshment spot en route. None of the terrain is pushchair friendly, so backpack the toddler.

Starting points are given with map references and postcodes, because the latter are necessary for some car-borne navigation systems, including that used by an ambulance crew who told me

they were 15 minutes late in arriving at an emergency because no postcode was given.

Direction details specify compass points which, clockwise, are N (north), NNE (north-northeast), E (east), ESE (east-southeast), SE (south-east), SSE (south-southeast), S (south), SSW (south-southwest), SW (south-west), WSW (west-southwest), W (west), WNW (west-northwest), NW (north-west) and WNW (west-northwest). The general direction can be assumed to remain the same until another compass point is given. Carry a compass.

Routes are along public rights of way or across access land. Both categories may be subject to change or diversion. Remember that conditions under foot will vary greatly according to the season and the weather. Do not set off if coastal fog ('sea fret' they call it) is likely.

Parking spaces are specified on the assumption that many walkers will

arrive by car or bicycle. Where public transport is mentioned, there were options currently available, but check with the provider before setting off and always make sure you also know the time of the last bus or train.

The Maps

Though we give a self-contained potted description of each walk you may need a map or global positioning system to find its parking point. Our sketch maps can only be a rough guide. A detailed map will prove useful if you stray from the route or are forced to cut the walk short. Remember that problems on the day may range from heat exhaustion to sea-fret or hill fog.

Two large-scale Ordnance Survey maps currently cover the south-east Devon area. They are Explorer 115 (Exmouth & Sidmouth) and Explorer 116 (Lyme Regis & Bridport). For availability, access www.ordnancesurvey.co.uk/leisure.

Level of difficulty:

Easy 🍂

Moderate 🍂 🍂

More challenging 🍂 🍂 🍂

Map symbols:

🚗   Park & start

〰️〰️〰️   Tarred Road

▪ ▪ ▪   Unpaved road

– – –   Footpath

■   Building

+   Church

▲   Triangulation pillar or other landmark

🚻   WC

🍴   Refreshments

🍺   Pub

Walk Locations

A30

Honiton

River Axe

A35

A30

River Otter

A375

River Sid

Exeter

A3052

5

A3052

Lyme Regis

4   **6**   **7**   **8**   **9**   **10**

A376

Sidmouth

Seaton

BEER HEAD

LANDSLIPS NATIONAL NATURE RESERVE

Exe Estuary

2   **3**

1

Budleigh Salterton

L Y M E   B A Y

Exmouth

ORCOMBE POINT

1 Littleham and Exmouth

Historic village and the main coastal centre linked by cliffs, National Trust fields and an old railway line, in a 7.5-mile circuit

Exmouth was a mediaeval port and can claim to be the oldest sea-bathing town in Devon. Georgian Exmouth amounts to a fashionable cluster of homes facing seawards from The Beacon. Regency Exmouth follows with Holy Trinity Church, oversized in 1824 and enlarged since, and Victorian terraces surround them. The latest arrivals have turned the former dockland peninsula into a futuristic high-rise dormitory. Coastline communities include historic Littleham and a one of great Devon caravan parks, separated from Exmouth by a National Trust buffer zone.

Level: 🐾
Length: 7.5 miles
Terrain: Easy and almost flat at the heart of the holiday coast.
Park and Start: In Littleham, below St Margaret's Church in Castle Road.
Start ref: SY 029 813
Postcode: EX8 2RL
Public Transport: Trains and buses to Exmouth where you can join the circuit en route
Websites: www.exmouth-guide.co.uk
www.jurassiccoast.com

Phear Park
Littleham Cross
11
Littleham
9
10
Clinton Arms
West Down Lane
8
Albion Hill
7
1
6 Exmouth
5
Esplanade
Devon Cliffs Holiday Park
Sandy Bay
High Land of Orcombe
Beachcomber Cafe Bar
2
4
3
Queen's Drive
Rifle Range
Rodney Point
Orcombe Point   LYME BAY   Straight Point
EXE ESTUARY
500m

7

Sula on stilts

1 Set off from the junction beside the churchyard, along West Down Lane (SE) to pass the public toilets, the Clinton Arms and Ye Olde Tythe Cottage tea-room. Continue straight ahead from Rodney Close to Devon Cliffs Holiday Park in 750 metres. Head for the sea, passing to the right of West Down Farm, to the cliff path above Littleham Cove in 500 metres.

Though ravaged by the Danes in AD 1003, Exmouth port remained important enough to supply 10 ships and 193 men for Edward III's expedition to Calais in 1347, and had a dock railway until December 1967.

2 Turn right (SW) and skirt the landward boundary of Straight Point Rifle Range. Turn right (W) on reaching the clifftop beyond the military fence in 1,000 metres. Follow signs along the seaward side of Beachcomber Café Bar above Sandy Bay.

3 In 1,000 metres the coast path crosses the High Land of Orcombe where the wild undercliff is known as The Floors. National Trust land extends down into the valley at Prattshayes. In a further 1,000 metres the cliff path rounds Orcombe Point and then Rodney Point.

Exmouth marina

Exe Estuary

(4) Follow the cliff path through scrub on the slope of Foxholes Hill. Join the cliff road and continue downhill to the cross-roads in 750 metres.

(5) Join Queen's Drive, beside the sand dunes, towards the Exe Estuary and the Inshore Rescue Boat Station in 750 metres. Continue ahead along the Esplanade for 1,000 metres, to the main Lifeboat Station in 1,000 metres.

The ancient church at Littleham – originally for Exmouth as well – boasts a lectern dating from 1250 which was carved from a beam from Salisbury Cathedral, beside one of Devon's finest rood screens.

Dawlish Ferry

Exe Estuary to Dawlish Warren which was Dickens's setting for the opening of *Nicholas Nickleby*.

7 Bear right (E) along Langerwehe Way to the roundabout, Pierhead and the Strand in 500 metres. Continue through the town centre, along Albion Street and up Albion Hill to Claremont Gardens in 750 metres.

The Drake family came from Spratte Hayes (now Prattshayes) and built Drake's aisle along the north side of Littleham church in 1526.

6 Bear right (N) to skirt around Exmouth Docks — now a yacht marina — for 500 metres to Shelly Road, the Ropewalk, and Camperdown Terrace. The last working slipways face The Point. Futuristic nautical architecture looks across the

Esplanade dunes

Orcombe Point

Lady Nelson, the admiral's
estranged widow, lived at
red-brick No. 6 The
Beacon in Exmouth and is
buried behind railings in
the seaward corner of
Littleham churchyard.

Straight Point

8 Turn left (N), down Marlpool Hill, to Phear Park in 600 metres.

9 Turn right (E), beside the cycle-way, with the landward part of Exmouth to the left and the seaward half to the right. Exit from the far right-hand corner of the park in 600 metres. Here the path and cycle-way join the course of a disused railway, following it into a cutting, and out of town to Littleham Cross and Littleham Road in 700 metres.

10 Proceed along the road towards Littleham for 600 metres and then turn left to re-join the track of the old railway.

11 Follow it for 600 metres. Now turn right, out of the cutting and then down into a valley, to return to St Margaret's Church at Littleham in a further 600 metres.

Ye Olde Tithe Cottage

High Land of Orcombe

Anne Isabella, Lady Byron, lived in Exmouth at Italianate No. 5 The Beacon.

2 Budleigh Salterton and East Budleigh

A 7-mile circuit that is high on history as well as the cliff-line.

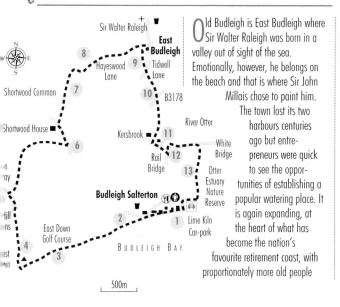

Old Budleigh is East Budleigh where Sir Walter Raleigh was born in a valley out of sight of the sea. Emotionally, however, he belongs on the beach and that is where Sir John Millais chose to paint him.

The town lost its two harbours centuries ago but entrepreneurs were quick to see the opportunities of establishing a popular watering place. It is again expanding, at the heart of what has become the nation's favourite retirement coast, with proportionately more old people

Level:

Length: 7 miles

Terrain: A couple of stiff climbs but otherwise easy tracks.

Park and Start: At Budleigh Salterton in the seaside Lime Kiln car-park at the eastern end of Budleigh Bay.

Start ref: SY 072 020

Postcode: EX9 6EP

Public Transport: Buses from Exmouth to Sidmouth.

Websites: www.devon.gov.uk
www.visitbudleigh.com

than can be found anywhere in the kingdom. Its name is a reminder that salt used to come from brine-boiling operations in the salterns. Large circular pebbles, known as cobbles, used to be lifted from the shore and became a characteristic local building stone.

Budleigh Salterton

Chit Rocks in Western Town mark the site of a thirteenth-century harbour, much like the Cobb at Lyme Regis, which was washed away by gales.

1 Set off along the seafront and Salting Hill (W) to Marine Parade and South Parade in 750 metres.

2 Bear left (SW), following signs for Clinton Walkway and the coast path, as the B3178 bends inland. Climb the cliffs of Western Town, above the site of Chit Rocks harbour, and leave Budleigh after Redcliff Court and Northview Road in 1,000 metres.

3 The path rises beside East Devon Golf Course to the Ordnance Survey pillar on West Down Beacon, at 424 feet above the sea, in a further 1,000 metres.

4 Turn right (N), inland beside the fence along the ridge, and follow this above Knowle Hill Plantations which cover the left-hand slope. Continue straight ahead on reaching the trees in 1,200 metres. Join Castle Lane which heads towards the B3178.

Walking the cycleway

5 Turn left (W) beside the railway bridge in 200 metres, down a slope for a further 200 metres, and join the Clinton Cycleway. Turn right (NE), into the cutting and under the bridge, and follow it to Bears Lane in 2,000 metres.

6 Turn left (NW), over the bridge, and pass Shortwood House and grounds in 400 metres. Continue straight ahead, down into the dip in 150 metres and bear right (N) to climb Shortwood Lane to hilltop Shortwood Common in 350 metres.

Sir Walter Raleigh (1552-1618) was born in Hayes Barton, a thatched Tudor farmhouse at the far end of Hayes Lane at East Budleigh.

(7) Continue straight ahead across the access land, between the pines, for 300 metres. Keep straight on, following the hedgerow which is to your right, down to Hayeswood Lane in 200 metres.

(8) Turn right (E) along this green lane which descends into East Budleigh in 1,500 metres. The track joins Middle Street opposite Drake's Primary School where we turn sharply right (SW) beside the frontage

Iconic moment

Another old railway

of Wynards Farmhouse and immediately uphill into a sandy hollow.

(9) Turn right at the junction with Tidwell Lane in 400 metres and then left (S) in 75 metres into a double-hedged green lane.

All Saints' Church at East Budleigh has 63 Tudor bench-ends with Raleigh links being commemorated by 1537-dated family coat of arms but what looks like 'the head of an American Red Indian' is now regarded as an English mythical Green Man.

Sir John Millais set up his easel on Budleigh beach, beside South Parade, to paint the 'Boyhood of Raleigh' which he exhibited to public acclaim at the Royal Academy in 1870.

10 Proceed with care from a concealed junction with the B3178 in 600 metres. Cross to the green lane on the other side.

11 Fork right on approaching Kersbrook in 200 metres and drop down into the hamlet in a further 200 metres. Turn left (SE), down to the junction in 150 metres, and turn right at the corner. Walk uphill, under the railway bridge, and then up

East Budleigh

steps to East Budleigh Road in 150 metres.

12 Cross the grass to South Farm Road and turn left (N), downhill and around the corner, to cross the flood plain (E) to White Bridge in 600 metres.

13 Turn right (S) along the causeway path between the River Otter to the left and marshes and a mere to the right. This is Devon Wildlife Trust's Otter Estuary Nature Reserve. Return to the seaside car-park in 1,000 metres.

Swan on the Otter

3 **Otterton and Danger Point**

A 7.5-mile circuit of the peninsula parish of Otterton with Lyme Bay on one side and the River Otter on the other.

Separated from Budleigh Salterton by the River Otter and its often fast-flowing tidal estuary, the sparsely-populated peninsula extends inland to the picturesque village of Otterton. In the other direction, above Ladram Bay, the red sandstone cliffs have produced spectacular free-standing offshore stacks. It is a pure chocolate-box seascape provided you blink on glancing towards the mobile homes and other cliffside facilities.

Monastic place-names above Ladram Bay preserve the memory of a Benedictine Priory established as a cell of the Abbey of Mount St Michael in Normandy.

Level:
Length: 7.5 miles
Terrain: Almost flat and generally undemanding.
Park and Start: In the vicinity of the King's Arms Hotel and thatched Basclose Farmhouse in Fore Street at Otterton.
Start ref: SY 081 853
Postcode: EX9 7HB
Public Transport: Buses from Budleigh Salterton to Bicton and Sidmouth.
Websites: www.devon.gov.uk
www.otterton.org.uk

Military buildings on Brandy Head overlooked a live-firing range used for the evaluation and testing of gun and rocket systems for fighter aircraft.

Otterton village

1 Set off beside The Green (W) and then turn left (S) in 100 metres between Millside Cottage and the Craft Centre. Walk up Church Hill, passing 1870-dated St Michael's Church, and turning left (E) below the churchyard griffin into Green Close in 150 metres.

2 Turn right in 100 metres, up Maunder's Hill, and then left into Behind Hayes. Proceed for 400 metres.

3 Turn right (S) just beyond the junction at Pepper's Corner, uphill into a green lane immediately after Lea Cottage. This is Lea Lane which we follow around to the left (E) on reaching a hilltop gate in 500 metres. In 400 metres it brings us to Stantyway Road.

Churchyard griffin

Ladram Rock

(5) Turn right (E) in 500 metres, opposite the equestrian entrance to Faraway. Follow the signs to Ladram Bay, into leafy Lower Ladram Lane which passes a 2006-dated post-modern Huf Haus. The track joins Bay Road for the final descent, in 1,000 metres, to Three Rocks Inn and Ladram Rock slipway in Ladram Bay.

Brandy Head is named for the smugglers who hauled kegs up the precipitous cliff but nearby Danger Point carries a keep-away message for shipping – warning of exposed ledges with variable tidal currents.

Seaside pigs

(4) Turn left (N) and then right and then left in 50 metres, opposite 1885-dated Stantyway Farm at Stantyway Cross. Take the untarred double-hedged track which is Piscombe Lane.

Danger Point

8 The hazard to avoid is in 300 metres where the tidal outlet of the River Otter can be fast flowing in both directions. Here the path bears right (N), keeping Budleigh Salterton across the water, with the space between being Otter Estuary Nature Reserve. A path leads to its bird hide.

6 Turn right (SW) opposite the thatched cottage. Hereon keep the sea to the left and fields to the right to leave caravan country beside Smallstones Point in 500 metres.

7 In 2,000 metres the coast path passes a wartime Observation Post on Brandy Head. The next landmark, a timber post, is in 1,500 metres on Danger Point. That is named for its hazards to shipping rather than ramblers.

John Leland, on a nation-wide tour in 1540, recorded that the Otter Estuary was still a functioning haven though as it was silting-up fewer than a hundred ships could use it

Otters and a long list of birds find a refuge in the reedy marshes of the extensive Otter Estuary Nature Reserve though dog-bothering has become a growing problem in recent years.

(9) In 1,000 metres the peninsula path joins South Farm Road. Turn left along it (W) and cross White Bridge in 200 metres.

(10) Turn right on the other side, keeping the river to your right, and pass Clamour Bridge in 1,500 metres. Continue to follow the river bank for a further 1,500 to Otterton Bridge. Turn right, passing Otterton Mill, to return to Fore Street.

River Otter

4 Mutter's Moor and Ladram

A 4.5-mile walk across high cliffs and the southern-most extremity of the Devon heaths

Peak Hill and High Peak live up to their names with perfect views of Sidmouth in its sylvan bowl.

The plateau on the landward side comprises open access pebblebed heathland which is managed as a nature reserve. Cliffside woods are owned by the National Trust. The walk also approaches prime herring gull territory in caravan country around the fantastic deep-red sandstone columns of Sandy Cove and Ladram Bay. The equal of Clovelly in North Devon and Lulworth in Dorset, Ladram was celebrated by the Romantic Movement and has been at the receiving end of mass tourism since Victorian times.

Level: 🥾 🥾
Length: 4.5 miles
Terrain: Ups and downs but otherwise easy.
Park and Start: In Mutter's Moor car-park beside the coast road a mile westwards out of Sidmouth, at the top of Peak Hill.
Start ref: SY 110 872
Postcode: EX10 6RZ
Public Transport: Buses to Sidmouth.
Websites: www.geograph.org.uk
www.worldheritagecoast.net

25

Mutter's Moor is named for Abraham Mutter who with fellow smuggler Jack Rattenbury hid caches of contraband here during the French Wars at the turn of the nineteenth century.

1 Set off across the road (S) to the National Trust's Peak Hill woodland, to the left of the field gate. Stay on the grassy top path through the trees until you reach a sandy track above the cliffs in 500 metres.

2 Turn right (SW), uphill, into the pasture and climb the coast path up Windgate slope. Continue up and over the wooded High Peak where the trees conceal a small Iron Age fort on the 515-feet summit in 1,300 metres.

3 Descend to Sandy Cove and Ladram Bay in 1,000 metres. Turn right (N) in the holiday complex and then take the access road that is closest to the cliffs where you have just been walking. This is Ladram Road (NW).

Peak Hill Wood

High Peak in the clouds

4 Turn left beside Sea View Farm in 600 metres and then right, downhill, into double-hedged Chockenhole Lane in 50 metres.

5 Turn right (NE) at the junction of tracks in 500 metres into Little Chockenhole Lane. Fork left in a further 500 metres to cross the stream and then bear right up Holestone Lane.

Belonging to the Clinton Devon Estates, Mutter's Moor and its clumps of western gorse and cross-leaved heath, across a dry pebble-strewn ridge, is the habitat of nightjar, stonechat and stone-pipit.

Mutter's Moor

The Clinton name is writ large across great parts of Devon with the current head of the family being Gerard Neville Mark Fane Trefusis, 22nd Baron Clinton (born 1934) whose title dates from 1299.

6 Turn right (E) on joining tarred Pinn Lane in 600 metres.

7 Make sure you face oncoming traffic. Follow the road for 1,500 metres, passing Lower Pinn and Horstone, to the corner below a bracken-covered slope.

8 Turn left (N) into a bridleway signed to Seven Stones and Bulverton Bottom. This ditch-side and then ravine-side Seven Stones Lane climbs on to common land at a gate above an old bottle dump in 400 metres. Proceed to the path junction in 100 metres on Mutter's Moor. This was the site of the prehistoric Seven Stones which was destroyed more than a century ago.

9 Turn right (E) along the grassy track to the closest pine wood in 150 metres.

10 Turn right (S), along the gravel road beside Greystone Hill Plantations, to return to the car-park in 700 metres.

The seaward side of Peak Hill was given to the National Trust in 1986 by Miss Anne Farewell Jones and the Sid Vale Association.

Ladram Bay was also famous for a natural arch until it collapsed to coastal erosion in 1925.

High Peak disappearing

Seven Stones Lane

5 Harpford and Bowd

A 6-mile walk, inland from the coastal belt, across Sidmouth's heathy hinterland

High ground inland of Sidmouth climaxes in wild heathland across the pebblebed plateau of Harpford Common. Harpford is an attractive village between there and the River Otter. Bowd Inn is an ancient thatched hostelry. Benchams and Harpford House are the local mansions in the green hinterland behind the coastal hills. This is one of those rare walks where one is spoilt for choice. The right of way returns to Harpford through a wooded ravine but the

Level: 🐾 🐾
Length: 6 miles
Terrain: Hill country with well-marked paths.
Park and Start: In Lower Way at Harpford where there are a couple of laybys towards Bridge End and the A3052 on east side of the River Otter.
Start ref: SY 092 899
Postcode: EX10 0NQ
Public Transport: Buses between Newton Poppleford and Sidford.
Websites: www.bestpubs.co.uk
www.ukvillages.co.uk

adjacent alternative is along the course of the seaside railway from Sidmouth, still scenic though without steam or trains, and now back in service as a permissive bridleway.

Harpford

1 Set off away from the main road (N) to the parish church of St Gregory the Great in 500 metres.

2 Turn left in Higher Way, uphill for 75 metres, and then right (E) between Littlecott Cottage and Peeks House into Knapp's Lane. Bear left in 150 metres, uphill, to pass Owlshayes and Hayes. Cross the bridge over an old railway line in 150 metres and continue straight ahead up a green lane which turns into a deep-cut sandy track. It is a long green tunnel in summertime.

A mediaeval court-leet met at Court Place, Harpford, which is said to have been the county gaol before cells were built at Bicton.

(3) Turn right (E) in 700 metres, on entering the open hilltop. Follow the hedgerow. Keep it to your right.

(4) Enter the beech wood in 300 metres and turn left. Turn right in 400 metres, on reaching the steps to the road, away from Wood's Farm and below the Recycling Centre. Ignore the first gates on to the road in 200 metres but turn left at the junction of tracks in a further 50 metres.

(5) Cross the road (NE) and follow signs to the Fire Beacon. Head towards the hilltop and climb across the pastures to a road beside the wood in 350 metres.

(6) Turn right (SE) for 100 metres. Now turn left (E), upwards, through the trees. Follow the blue bridleway signs and turn sharply left (NW) in 250 metres. Climb to the summit of heathy Harpford Common, in 300 metres, with a view over Sidmouth and Lyme Bay. This is Beacon Hill. The main track (NW) crosses the plateau for 500 metres, with Fire Beacon Plantation across to the left, and then becomes a track.

through the broad-leaved trees of Core Wood which is owned by the Woodland Trust.

Fire Beacon Wood

Bulverton view

'Rock of Ages' hymn-writer Revd Augustus Toplady, vicar of Harpford in 1766-68, is commemorated on the restored thirteenth-century churchyard cross.

(7) On the other side of this wood, in 400 metres, Hollow Head Cross is a hilltop cross-roads of tracks with a stone inscribed 'SD' and a traffic restriction sign. Turn right here (SE), downhill, into a green lane which heads towards Sidford for 1,000 metres.

(8) Turn right (SW) on reaching the road to Burscombe Farm with Sidbury Castle earthworks on the wooded plateau beyond. Follow the path – in opposite direction – up to a

The railway from Sidmouth Junction, near Honiton, to Tipton St John and seaside Sidmouth opened on 6 July 1874 but the station was built a mile inland because the select resort wished to discourage trippers.

Harpford Common

Hollow Head

projecting corner of the wood in 100 metres, uphill in the field for a further 50 metres, and go through the gate into the trees.

9 From the summit of Core Hill, in 100 metres, our descent is into a sunken trackway, straight ahead to the road in a further 100 metres.

10 Turn left (S) left, downhill, to the second path sign just before the drive to the house in 150 metres. Turn right (SW), down into the pasture to a point below the front windows. Turn left across a stile in 150 metres, into a green lane, and then right just around the corner in 25 metres.

11 Keep the fence to your left and Saltwynds Farm to the right. Proceed straight ahead here, in 500 metres, along its drive. This is Saltways Lane.

12 Also proceed straight ahead at the road junction with Fire Beacon Lane in 400 metres. Continue to the next road junction in 300 metres.

Core Hill Wood

13 Turn left and then immediately right at an old railway bridge. A short diversion to the left

Sidbury Castle Hill

brings you to the 1651-dated thatched Bowd Inn.

14　Our onward route (W) is along the preserved track-bed of a section of the disused railway from Sidmouth to Sidmouth Junction,

Bowd Inn

beyond Ottery St Mary. Follow the permissive bridleway along the track through the trees, though you do have the option of an alternative path down to the left in Harpford Wood, and follow the stream in the gully. The public footpath also leads to Harpford in 2,000 metres.

15　Beyond the wood, the railway option continues straight ahead between sandy fields. Then turn right between Harpford No. 9 Bore Hole and bridge 'Sid 13'. Cross this, over the top, and walk down the lane into the village.

Pedestrian railway

Dr Richard Beeching's mass closure of branch railway lines caught up with the Sidmouth section (to Tipton St John, Ottery St Mary and Sidmouth Junction) on 8 May 1967.

6 Sidmouth and Salcombe Regis

A relatively tough 5 miles sampling a wide variety of National Trust landscapes

Regency Sidmouth is still a delight. It is a miniature Brighton with pastel-coloured cottage ornées between the sea and the River Sid which is graced by a ribbon of public parks and meadows. Young Princess Victoria would have remembered it for the moment in 1820 when her destiny became clear. Elderly playwright George Bernard Shaw spent 1938 being ill at the Victoria Hotel where he used the fire escape to avoid seeing other guests. GBS took no notice of bluebells or other natural beauties and would be oblivious to the present-day abundance of National Trust omega signs. These are thanks to the generous gifts of local residents and altruistic fund-raising by the Sid Vale Association. The group itself also owns some fields. As a result the place is amazingly access-friendly.

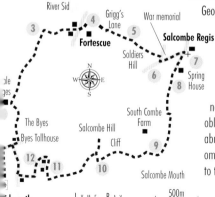

Level: 🐾 🐾
Length: 5 miles
Terrain: Ups and downs through heritage countryside.
Park and Start: In Sidmouth, either on-street or in a car-park off East Street.
Start ref: SY 127 874
Postcode: EX10 8BL
Public Transport: Buses between Exeter and Lyme Regis.
Websites: www.devon.gov.uk
www.sidmouth.gov.uk

Byes Bridge Tollhouse

Beside the bridge over the River Sid, the 1817-dated Byes Tollhouse is an exquisite Greek Revival style cottage ornée.

1 Set off along Millford Road or Salcombe Road and cross the River Sid to Byes Tollhouse. Turn left (N) beside its gate, into The Byes, a long strip of riverside open space. Proceed straight ahead, passing the

Regency Sidmouth

waterfall, to enter National Trust parkland after a pair of huge holm oaks.

2 Continue to the second crossing of the river, which is Sid Lane Bridge, in 1,000 metres. Cross it and turn immediately right beside Sid Vale

Cottages. Follow the hedgerow of Margaret's Meadow to the far side of the second pasture in 600 metres.

3 Turn right (E) at the crossroads of paths to a bridge over the river and then up through the gates

Sid Vale Cottages

While staying at Woolbrook Cottage (now Royal Glen Hotel) in January 1820 young Princess Victoria learnt of the deaths of both her grandfather (King George III) and her father (Duke of Kent), which reduced her separation from the British throne to three childless uncles.

into Fortescue hamlet in 400 metres. Walk up to the main road in 400 metres and turn left (N) along it.

4 Turn right (SE) in 150 metres, up Grigg's Lane which becomes a farm track. It leads to a junction of

paths in 600 metres. Go through the gate and climb the woodland option, straight ahead up and over Soldier's Hill.

5 Emerge from the trees into a pasture in 300 metres. There is

gorse scrub to the left and a hilltop water-tank to the right. This is the James Cornish Field which was given to the Sid Vale Association by Mrs M. M. Page in 1977. Across the fields to the right is the Norman Lockyer Observatory from where asteroid D0111 was photographed making a 290,000-miles near miss of Earth in March 2009.

Fishing at Fortescue

Before marrying Robert
Browning, poet Elizabeth
Barrett (1806-61) lived in
Fortfield Terrace, Sidmouth,
and All Saints Road — now
Cedar Shade Residential
Home — where she
translated Aeschylus's
Prometheus Bound in
1833.

to your left, for 1,000 metres, to
Salcombe Mouth.

6 Turn right at the road in 200 metres and then immediately left, beside the War Memorial, to pass Combe Head and Rock Cottage.

7 Descend into the valley in 300 metres and turn right (S) beside Salcombe Regis Church.

8 Walk down the road to Spring House in 200 metres and take the second path on the right, opposite the magnolia at its garden gate. Then follow the valley path across National Trust land below hillside Combe Wood Farm (to the left) and Southcombe Farm (up to the right). Keep the stream

9 Turn right (W) to begin the ascent of Salcombe Hill Cliff. Follow Sidmouth signs up the slope and climb its 188 steps. Stay on the cliff path up and over the plateau for 900 metres to the stone commemorating the gift of the land to the National Trust.

Hill Observatory above Sidmouth was established in 1910 by the astronomer Sir Norman Lockyer (1836-1920) who led nine eclipse expeditions around the globe between 1870 and 1905 and discovered helium in the solar atmosphere.

Proceed to the topograph and seats on the other side of the hedge.

Combe Wood Farm

(10) Here we turn right and then left, into the sycamore wood, from where it is downhill all the way to Sidmouth in 800 metres. Take the signed options closest to the cliffs but follow any diversions around landslips.

(11) Turn right (N) on reaching the pasture beside the first houses to the Rocket House at the top of Laskeys Lane in 200 metres. Continue straight ahead at the corner into the alleyway, around to Cliff Road.

(12) Leave the coast path at Overthorpe in 500 metres. Either turn left (S) to cross the Sid estuary footbridge into Eastern Town or turn right (N) along Beatlands Road, with the river beneath trees to the left, to Sunnycroft and Willow Bridge Hotel in

National Trust cliffs

500 metres. Cross Millford Road to return to the Byes Tollhouse.

Vaughan Cornish gave Southcombe Farm and Salcombe Hill to the National Trust in 1937 and carved a commemoration: 'No sounds of worldly toil ascending there, admire the full in burst of prayer.'

7 Salcombe Regis and Dunscombe

Short and simple, across 4 miles of mainly National Trust land, plus donkeys galore

Donkeys seem to outnumber people in these parts though they also attract a disproportionate number of visitors. Salcombe Regis is a tranquil gem though a large sign has threatened development. One hopes that nimbyism is alive and active in this sheltered glen. As for the cliffs they are mostly safe and secure in National Trust ownership. Combe Wood Farm is particularly delightful. Its V-shaped valley has sheltered sides but seawards it becomes elemental. There is a grantite memorial in the churchyard to the astronomer Sir Norman Lockyer — buried here — who established the Hill Observatory on the plateau above the village and died in 1920.

Level: 🥾 🥾
Length: 4 miles
Terrain: One coastal climb but not otherwise strenuous.
Park and Start: From the car-park below the churchyard at Salcombe Regis.
Start ref: SY 148 888
Postcode: EX10 0JN
Public Transport: Buses along the main road from Exeter to Lyme Regis.
Websites: www.thedonkeysanctuary.org.uk
www.francisfrith.com/salcombe regis

Donkey Sanctuary

Salcombe Regis

Slade House Farm

Field of Dreams

Combe Wood Farm

Dunscombe Cliff

Lincombe

Dunscombe Coppice

Weston Mouth

Salcombe Mouth

500m

LYME BAY

43

Salcombe Regis Church

A fourteenth-century lectern, carved with a chough (or some other corvid) was hidden during the Reformation under the thatch of Sid Abbey and taken to Salcombe Regis when the church was restored in 1849.

(1) Set off up the lane, beside St Mary and St Peter's Church, and turn right (E) in 100 metres. Follow the road uphill beside the thatched Old School and leave the village in 250 metres. Ignore the first footpath sign on the left but cross the next stile (N) in 100 metres.

(2) Turn right (E) on the other side of the field in 200 metres. Turn left and then right to cross another path in 400 metres. Proceed to the Donkey Sanctuary in a further 400 metres.

(3) Turn left at the road and then immediately right into a corridor between donkey paddocks.

(4) Turn right (S) on reaching the track below Slade House Farm (with its donkey pens and feeding troughs) in 200 metres. Go through the Field of Dreams and then beside and through Dunscombe Coppice to descend beside the stream to Weston Mouth in 1,500 metres.

Donkey Sanctuary

Weston options

Weston Mouth

(5) Turn right (NW), from 1930-dated Glen chalet, and climb Lower Dunscombe Cliff towards Dunscombe. Then turn left

The Donkey Sanctuary around Slade House Farm was founded by Dr Elisabeth Svendsen in 1969 and in now one of ten such farms that have provided a refuge for more than 12,000 donkeys and mules.

to follow the coastal path which curves inland across National Trust land to skirt bowl-shaped Lincombe in 800 metres. Having turned again (SW) towards the sea the path climbs the high plateau of Higher Dunscombe Cliff.

Weston beach paths

The geology starts to change as the old red sandstone becomes overlaid by white chalk comprising trillions of microscopic fossils laid down from Cretaceous sea life.

Dunscombe crags

The coast path was walked by Coast Guards until 1913 and watched by the military during two world wars, particularly from June 1940 when it was defended by barbed wire, minefields, pillboxes and anti-tank obstacles.

6 In 1,000 metres, on reaching the edge of the valley above Salcombe Mouth, we turn right (N) for 150 metres and then descend National Trust slopes to the thatched and Regency buildings of Combe Wood Farm in 500 metres.

7 Follow its access road into the valley beside Spring House in 600 metres. Bear right, uphill, to return to the car-park in 200 metres.

Combe Wood Farm

8 Weston and Street

A 6-mile circuit in deep-cut valleys, with wooded slopes, and along high cliffs

Tucked away in deep-cut valleys, the hamlets of Edge, Hole and Street have simple names that are pure description. Each has precipitous slopes, with those at Edge bearing having a sunny platform with an historic house, while its equivalent at Hole is deep down in the shadows. Other cottages were associated with mills which were powered by the fast-moving streams. Street is pure cottage vernacular clustering around a spring-side inn. It is a true fountain that gives the Fountain Head its name. As with

Level: 🐾 🐾
Length: 6 miles
Terrain: Pleasantly up and down.
Park and Start: In Weston, in the car-park at Lower Weston Farm, which is beside the post-box.
Start ref: SY 167 890
Postcode: EX10 0PH
Public Transport: None supplied
Websites: www.nationaltrust.org.uk
www.ukvillages.co.uk

many of these walks there are plenty of National Trust pastures en route – including Berry Cliff – with an Iron Age settlement at Berry Camp.

Edge Farm
Edge House
Edge Barton
Linhay
Ashton
Hole House
Grammar Lane
eston
Lower Weston
Fountain Head Inn **Street**
Berry Camp
Coxe's Cliff
Weston Combe
Ramshorn Rock   Chimney Rock   500m
L Y M E   B A Y

Edge Barton

Nicholas Wadham (1532-1609), the founder of Wadham College, Oxford, came from Edge Barton Manor where he was one of twenty children.

1 Set off uphill, turning left (N) along the road, to pass Hornshayne and Jasmine Cottage. Continue straight ahead at the junction in 200 metres. Walk the length of Grammar Lane.

2 Turn right (E) at the triple junctions in 500 metres. Proceed to the house at Ashton in 300 metres.

3 Turn left (N) immediately after the house, into the farm road, and bear right (NE) beside the barn and Ashton Farm Linhay. Follow the green lane, which then becomes a path, straight ahead beside the hedgerow to the road in 900 metres.

4 Cross this into the lane leading to Edge Farm in 500 metres. Bear right (SE), around the corner beside Edge House into the deep-cut valley. The road passes a range of cottages in 500 metres. Continue through the first gateway at

Hole cottages

Edge Barton Manor but bear right at the main gateway in 200 metres down a grassy track to a field gate below the mansion.

Hole House

5 Cross the pasture, down the slope to the far corner beyond the ponds in 300 metres. Go through both gates and cross the stream, which you now follow, keeping it to your left. The path emerges from behind the thatched Linhay at Hole Mill on to a tarred road. Turn right (S), steeply uphill, and then left in front of Hole House in 200 metres. Go through its gate piers.

6 Turn right halfway up the slope, in 150 metres, on to a bridleway up through wild garlic and scrub. This climbs the steep side of

Beehive Cottage

Underground mines between Beer and Branscombe produced the creamy limestone from which Exeter Cathedral was built between 1275 and 1360.

49

The Fountain Head

Fountain Head Inn, with flagstones and a wonderful open fireplace, takes its name from the spring that gushes from the ground behind the building.

Hole Hill, into a beech wood, to a tarred road in 150 metres.

7 Turn left for 100 metres. Go through the gate beside the cattle-grid and then turn right (W), uphill, out of the valley beside the humps and hollows of Hole Pits stone workings. Bear right from the summit, down across a pasture and head for the lane on the other side of the valley. In 750 metres a green lane drops down to Fountain Head Inn.

Fountain Head fireplace

Above Branscombe

8 Cross the road and walk through the beer garden and car-park to the second lane in 50 metres. Turn left and then right (SE), 5 metres up from the chimney-breast of thatched Rookeries, to climb from its garden up the hillside pasture and enter National Trust land at Pit Coppice. Continue straight ahead to the coast path on Berry Cliff in 1,000 metres.

Trust stile at Weston

9 Turn right (W) and follow signs for Weston Mouth. Relatively slight earthworks belong to Iron Age Berry Camp. Below are cliff chalets, ending with Romany Van. The path curves inland around a dip at Coxe's Cliff in 1,000 metres. Proceed for the length of Weston Cliff, overlooking Strangman's Cove, to a path junction in a further 1,000 metres above Ramshorn Rock.

10 Turn right, inland, along the top of the big wooded valley at Weston Combe. Keep to the scrub on the high ground with fields to your right. Turn right, uphill, on reaching the farm road from the beach in 800 metres. This brings you to the car-park in 400 metres.

Berry Cliff

Shallow sea off Coxe's Cliff was chosen for 'beaching' the stricken and fully-loaded container ship MSC Napoli – 48 hours after the 42,000-tonne vessel foundered in the English Channel on 18 January 2007 – causing a two-year clearance operation.

Last of the Napoli

9 Beer and Branscombe

Five miles around the conspicuous transition from red to white cliffs

This is the other half of Branscombe – those deep-cut combes – plus Branscombe Mouth itself and the first (or last) self-respecting white cliff of old England that sea-travellers see. The National Trust presence includes three time-warp facilities that every village once took for granted – a corn-mill,

bakery and a smithy. Two are thatched and the forge is still in business after more than two centuries. Branscombe Bakery had the last faggot-fuelled oven in Devon, operated by brothers Gerald and Stuart Collier until 1987. It could have continued but fell foul of

Level: 🏵 🏵
Length: 5 miles
Terrain: Several long but relatively gradual climbs.
Park and Start: In Beer, in the car-park on Common Hill which is above Common Lane at the seaward southern extremity of the village.
Start ref: SY 228 888
Postcode: EX12 3AQ
Public Transport: Coastal buses via Seaton and Beer.
Websites: www.beer-devon.co.uk
www.worldheritagecoast.net

health and safety regulations, so is now a museum and tea-room. Up on the cliffs, Beer Head has perfect views of Lyme Bay from Start Point to Portland. Columns of chalk stand proud on the tumbled undercliff.

LYME BAY

Beer Head

1. Set off downhill, initially, but then turn sharp right (S) at the junction. Go up Little Lane for 300 metres. Turn left on approaching Beer Head Caravan Park to join the cliff path which skirts Arratt's Hill overlooking Beer Roads anchorage.

2. Proceed for 1,000 metres, with Pound's Pool Beach down to the left, on to the 426-feet high promontory of Beer Head which is the conspicuous western extremity of the famous chalk cliffs of the English Channel. Here the path and

Lace-making being a local cottage industry, Queen Victoria's wedding dress was made at Beer.

Chalk columns

(4) Here the onward path (NW) continues across National Trust land, between the café and the hotel, to climb West Cliff in 400 metres. There a tumbling mixture of undercliff and old quarries falls away to the left as the path follows a belt of woodland on the landward slope.

(5) Turn right (N) into the trees in 1,000 metres. Head for the

clifftop turn together (W). There are two options, either to bear left and follow the lower path through the undercliff and beech-huts of Under Hooken in 200 metres, or to stay on top and pass the former lookout and signal station on Hooken Cliffs in 500 metres.

(3) The upper path joins a bridleway which passes to the right of the buildings. In 600 metres it enters National Trust land on East Cliff from where we descend for the next 600 metres to join the undercliff path cliff at Branscombe Mouth.

Branscombe Church

An Elizabethan gallery and a rare eighteenth-century three-decker pulpit can be seen in St Winifred's Church at Branscombe, along with one of a series of mediaeval wall paintings featuring the Seven Deadly Sins ('Lust' alone survives).

battlements on the tower of St Winifred's Church. Cross the stream and walk up between two ancient yew trees in 300 metres.

6 Turn right (E) down the village street. Pass the Bakery and the Forge in 300 metres and turn right at the junction into Mill Lane. This leads to Manor Mill in 200 metres.

7 Continue straight ahead, along the valley path, for 300 metres. Turn left (N) at the path

Stone coffin at Branscombe

Floral Branscombe

junction, to return to the village opposite Ye Olde Mason's Arms in 250 metres.

8 Bear right and then turn left (NE), up the hill, to the next junction in 200 metres.

Admire Branscombe's floral displays at Country Cottage, Country House, Coombe Cottage and Longview.

Branscombe's valley

9 Turn right (E), but not into the narrow lane, and instead climb the path up through Hazelwood to Stockham's Hill in 300 metres. Follow the hedgerow straight ahead, keeping it to your left, for 300 metres. Bear right in the next field from where our path heads towards the left-hand side of a small wood in 200 metres.

10 Continue straight ahead for a further 200 metres. The path becomes Mare Lane which descends above Pecorama Pleasure Gardens to join Underlays in 1,200 metres.

11 Turn left for 75 metres and then turn right at the corner. This path between the houses crosses

Branscombe Forge, owned by the National Trust, is the last working thatched smithy in Britain.

the dip at Barline and then climbs up to Clapp's Lane in 150 metres. Cross Higher Meadows.

12 This brings us to Common Lane in 250 metres. Turn right, uphill, to return to the car-park in 100 metres.

Branscombe Mouth

Beer beach

10 Axmouth and Undercliffs

A demanding 11-mile expedition through the wildest landscape in Devon and Dorset

This walk comes with a caution. The landslipped undercliffs between Axmouth and Lyme Regis are not for the faint hearted. Flora and bird lists are impressive but hardly begin to catalogue the vast variety of species that live in conditions of almost total solitude and secrecy. Impenetrable is the word that doubly applies to most of the undulating ground for reasons of geology and vegetation. It it the wildest landscape in Devon and Dorset, arguably more difficult to cross than the western moors, though there is a waymarked path. This tends to be rough and

Level: 🥾 🥾 🥾
Length: 11 miles
Terrain: Long and tough with no opt-out from the Undercliffs.
Park and Start: From Axmouth village.
Start ref: SY 259 911
Postcode: EX12 4AN
Public Transport: Devon Bus current services are the X53 and 899 but check with their traveline on 0871 200 22 33.
Websites: www.jurassiccoast.com
www.seatonbay.com

ready and will be liable to change when the next landslip happens. There is a way to cheat on doing the full circuit — halve it by taking a taxi (or enlist a second car) to join it en route at Ware Farm. Telephone for a taxi from Seaton on 01297 20038 or 01297 23366 (www.clappstaxis.co.uk).

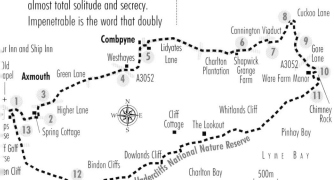

Cuckoo Lane
Cannington Viaduct
8
Combpyne
Lidyates Lane
Westhayes
5
Lidyates Lane
Charlton Plantation
Shapwick Grange Farm
6
7
9
Gore Lane
A3052
Ware Farm Manor
10
ur Inn and Ship Inn
Old apel
Axmouth
Green Lane
4
A3052
3
Higher Lane
2
Spring Cottage
13
Cliff Cottage
Whitlands Cliff
The Lookout
11
Chimney Rock
Pinhay Bay
Dowlands Cliff
Undercliffs National Nature Reserve
LYME BAY
12
Bindon Cliffs
Charlton Bay
500m
en Cliff

Axmouth and Undercliffs

Spring Cottage

1. Set off up Chapel Street (E), following it from the 1861-dated Old Chapel to the end of the village, after The Gatehouse in 1,000 metres.

2. Turn left opposite the entrance to Bindon Manor, uphill into a green lane. Then turn right (N) in 50 metres beneath the ash tree after thatched Spring

Cottage. Climb the wild hillside to Higher Lane in 200 metres.

3. Turn right (E) to continue uphill. Fork left at a triangle of grass in 300 metres. This green lane is actually called Green Lane. In 1,000 metres we continue straight ahead along a bitumen lane to the

A3052 at Heathfield Cross in 900 metres.

4. Cross to the entrance to Westhayes Caravan Park but then turn immediately right, through a gate, into the right-hand field. Pinewood Homes are behind the hedgerow to the left. Follow the path as it drops down to Combpyne Lane in the valley in 750 metres. Turn left (N) to the junction in the hamlet in 150 metres.

The oldest intact concrete bridge in England, the old Axmouth Bridge was in use from 1877 until replacement in 1990, and is now an ancient monument.

Stepps House

River Axe

Inland up the Axe Estuary, the Harbour Inn and Ship Inn at Axmouth are in the main street, opposite St Michael's Church.

7 Turn right, up to the corner in 100 metres, and turn left into a bridleway. This along the foot of Horseman's Hill into Cuckoo Lane in 750 metres.

5 Turn right (E), into and up Lidyates Lane, to the main road at Charlton Plantation in 1,500 metres. Cross into the lane on the other side which drops down to Shapwick Grange Farm in 1,000 metres.

6 Continue for a further 100 metres and then bear left across the pasture down to Cannington Lane beneath the concrete supports of Cannington Viaduct in 400 metres.

Cuckoo Lane

Axmouth Harbour

around to the top end of the pasture in 100 metres. Turn left here, across a stile, and follow the hedge to the stile in 150 metres.

10 Enter the Undercliffs National Nature Reserve and descend via viewpoint Chimney Rock to the main path above Underhill Farm in 150 metres.

Whitlands Landslip (3 February 1840)

8 Turn right (S), 10 metres after Cuckoo Hill Cottages, up steps into trees beside the garden and along the side of the hilltop field to Gore Lane in 500 metres.

Caption

9 Turn right and cross the A3052 in 500 metres. Proceed for 300 metres and turn right into the entrance to Ware Farm Manor. Then turn immediately left and follow the right-hand hedgerow

(11) Here we turn right (W) and become committed to the only public path through the wild undercliffs and their multiple landslips. Follow the yellow waymarks. The onward path is 7,500

Bindon Landslip

One landslip carried a field of corn into what is now the middle of the Undercliffs and another caused the seabed to heave up out of the water, while that at Dowlands on Christmas Eve in 1839 left a chasm 150 feet deep and 300 feet wide.

metres, via Ware Cliffs, Pinhay Cliffs, Whitlands Cliff, Annie's Cottage (ruin), Dowlands Cliff and Landslips and Culverhole Point.

(12) The final ascent is up wooded Bindon Cliffs to the fields on Haven Cliff. In 700 metres the path bears right (N), up and over the rise,

Chimney Rock

The Undercliffs National Nature Reserve, from Axmouth to Lyme Regis, covers 750 acres and is managed by Natural England.

Bindon skunk cabbage

with Axe Cliff Golf Course across to the left. Cross Barn Close Lane in 500 metres. Drop down to the stile in the hedgerow in 200 metres.

(13) Turn left (NW), down Stepps Road, to pass Parsonage Barn and return to the village in 600 metres.

> *Built in 1902, to carry a branch railway from Axminster to Lyme Regis from 1903 till 1965, the great concrete viaduct above Cannington Farm is 609 feet long and 93 feet high.*

Downlands Cliff

Estuary swan